DATE DUE			

ALIENS FROM EARTH
When ANIMALS and PLANTS INVADE Other ECOSYSTEMS

Written by Mary Batten
Illustrated by Beverly J. Doyle

PEACHTREE
ATLANTA

To the memory of Tier,
a dear aunt who always believed in me
—M. B.

To the struggling species
and the ever-shrinking habitats that support them
—B. J. D.

Ω

PEACHTREE PUBLISHERS
1700 Chattahoochee Avenue
Atlanta, Georgia 30318-2112

www.peachtree-online.com

Text © 2003, 2016 by Mary Batten
Illustrations © 2003, 2016 by Beverly J. Doyle

Book design by Loraine M. Joyner
Composition by Melanie McMahon Ives

Illustrations rendered in acrylic on clayboard. Title typeset in BulwarkNF by Nick Curtis for Nick's Fonts; subtitle typeset in Optima Bold from Adobe Systems Incorporated; text typeset in Goudy Infant from dtp Type Limited.

Printed in November 2015 by Imago in Singapore

10 9 8 7 6 5 4 3 2 1
Revised Edition

Library of Congress Cataloging-in-Publication Data
Batten, Mary.
  Aliens from Earth / written by Mary Batten ; illustrated by Beverly Doyle.-- revised ed.
    p. cm.
Summary: Explores how and why plants and animals enter ecosystems to which they are not native, as well as the consequences of these invasions for other animals, plants, and humans.
HC 978-1-56145-900-1
PB 978-1-56145-903-2
1. Biological invasions--Juvenile literature. [1. Animal introduction. 2. Plant introduction.] I. Doyle, Beverly, 1963- ill. II. Title.
QH353 .B29 2003
577'.18--dc21
                    2002013170

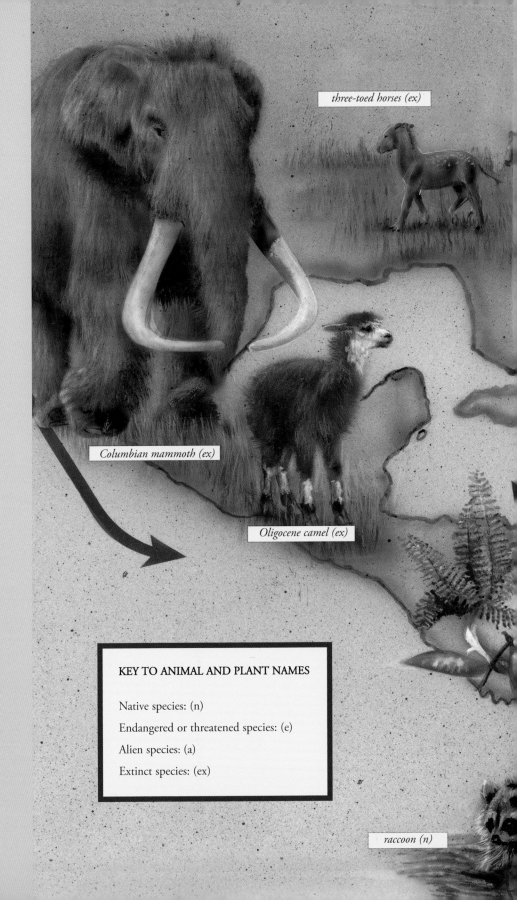

three-toed horses (ex)

Columbian mammoth (ex)

Oligocene camel (ex)

raccoon (n)

KEY TO ANIMAL AND PLANT NAMES

Native species: (n)

Endangered or threatened species: (e)

Alien species: (a)

Extinct species: (ex)

ALIENS ARE EVERYWHERE. These are not creatures from
other planets, but real living things right here on Earth.
Aliens are plants or animals that invade another ecosystem—
a natural community of plants and animals living in balance
with one another. Scientists call these aliens exotics, a word
that means "to come from outside." They are also called invasive species.

A healthy ecosystem needs biodiversity (a variety of
living organisms) and a balance between predators and prey.
Alien invaders can upset the balance of an ecosystem and
threaten its biodiversity.

For millions of years, living things traveled from one place
to another, but never so quickly as today. Throughout most of
Earth's long evolutionary history, animals walked, flew, and
crawled across ancient land bridges from one continent
to another. Carried by wind, water, birds, and other
animals, seeds moved from place to place. Over
thousands of centuries, ecosystems changed,
some species became extinct, and new
ones evolved, but the pace was slow.

giant sloth (ex)

capybara (n)

opossum (n)

glyptodon (ex)

titanis (ex)

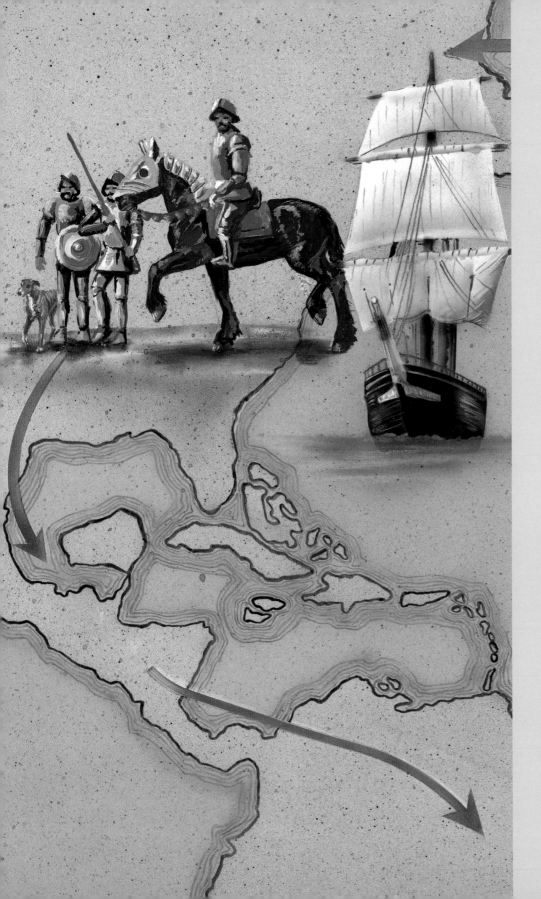

Humans greatly sped up the pace of alien invasions by becoming alien invaders themselves. The earliest humans evolved in Africa about a million and a half years ago. *Homo sapiens*, the species to which all modern people belong, appeared in Africa about 150,000 years ago. As their numbers grew, people began to need more natural resources. Eventually they moved into places where human beings had never lived before. They hunted animals, gathered native plants, and learned to farm. Wherever people settled, they changed the habitat.

Over the centuries, people invented ways to go longer distances and to move around faster. When people began traveling by ship, they took animals like goats, dogs, cats, and chickens with them, as well as the seeds of plants they wanted to grow. Unknowingly, they also took some stowaways like rats and mice. These migrations changed native ecosystems.

Today every living thing imaginable—viruses, bacteria, insects, plants, sea creatures—travels on the same planes and ships that carry people and cargo. Invaders move rapidly all over the globe. It is becoming harder to maintain the delicate balance in the world's ecosystems.

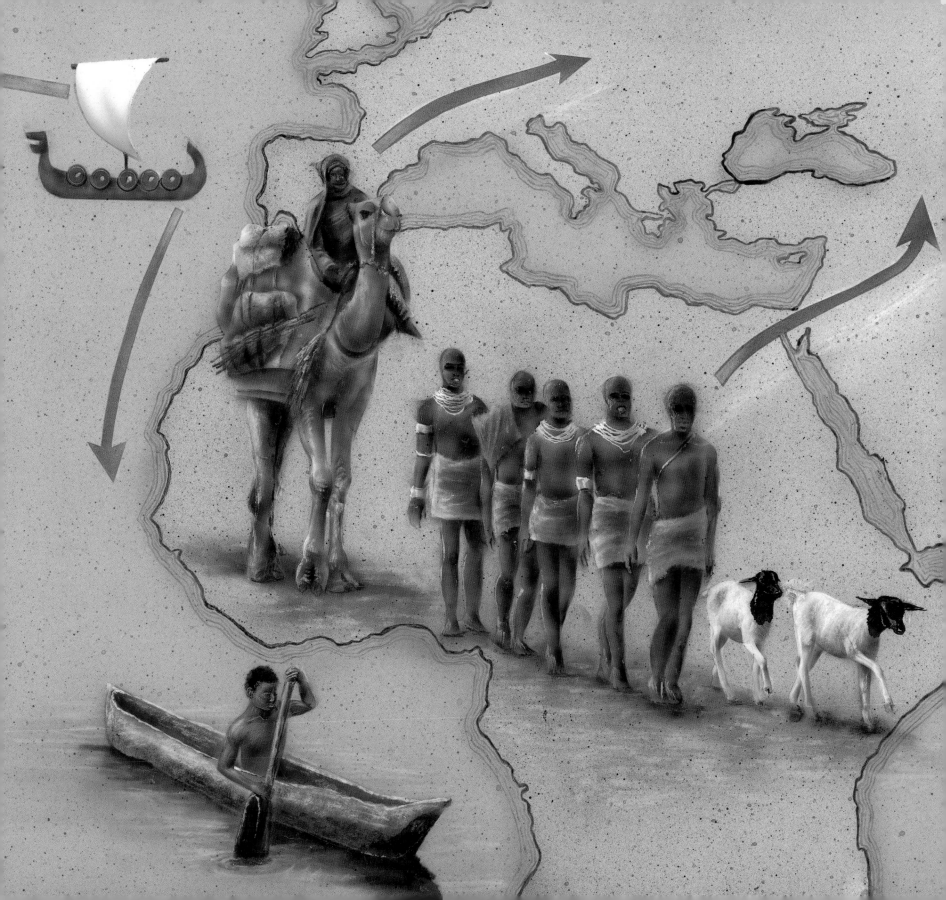

domestic sheep and cattle (a)

fox (a)

nombat (e)

ISLANDS ARE ESPECIALLY vulnerable to alien invasions.

Because they are surrounded by water, islands are cut off from other lands. Their native species have evolved in isolation and have not developed defenses to protect them from aliens. Until very recently in Earth's history, few new species were able to cross the miles of ocean to reach an island, but today every ship or plane that goes to an island may carry an alien invader. On islands worldwide, invasive species have driven many birds, mammals, and reptiles into extinction.

Even a large island continent like Australia can suffer damage from alien invasions.

koala (n)

cane toad (a)

domestic cat (a)

banded hare wallaby (e)

thylacine (ex)

burrowing bettong (e)

fox (a)

bridled nail-tail wallaby (e)

rabbit (a)

WHEN PEOPLE MIGRATE to new lands, alien species go with them.

More than 200 years ago, Europeans colonized Australia. Stowaway rats from their ships soon overran the countryside. Later settlers brought over cats to rid the fields of the rats. Because they encountered no predators, the cats multiplied quickly and threatened the survival of the native animals. As the numbers of these aliens increased, biodiversity decreased. The cats escaped into the wild and, with no natural enemies, grew big and fierce. Today they are about three times as large as house cats.

In the 1870s, the settlers introduced rabbits and foxes to hunt for sport. The foxes preyed on farm animals, and have now spread across three-quarters of the continent and cause more than two million dollars in damage each year. The foxes and the wild cats feasted on some of Australia's unique marsupials and ate them into extinction.

Today Australia has more than 500 million rabbits, sometimes called the world's "most ecologically damaging herbivore." These animals eat plants, destroy topsoil, damage farmers' crops, and wreck the habitat of many native species.

glider (n)

domestic cat (a)

Australian mala (e)

bilby (e)

brown rat (a)

po'ouli (e)

HAWAII, A STATE made up of islands, has been called the invasion capital of the world. Approximately twelve new plants and twenty-eight alien species of insects are accidentally introduced there every year.

European domestic pigs were among the earliest aliens introduced to Hawaii. Well suited to life in the islands' wet forests, their population grew rapidly. Some of them escaped into the wild, where they had a destructive effect on the rainforests. They rooted in the forest floor, digging up native trees and plants, which caused erosion and allowed invasive plants to replace native plants.

The pigs brought by early settlers dug at the starchy roots of native tree ferns and left behind hollow spots that collected rainwater. No one suspected that these little fern ponds would one day become a perfect habitat for mosquitoes, an insect that did not inhabit Hawaii at that time.

In 1826, when sailors from the whaling ship *Wellington* rinsed out their water barrels, they unknowingly dumped mosquito larvae into the fern ponds. The mosquitoes bred there quickly. These insects carried a blood parasite that caused malaria in native birds, killing off several species.

Many kinds of honeycreepers, Hawaii's most famous birds, are now extinct. Because of alien invasion and habitat destruction, the extinction rate of Hawaii's birds is the highest in the United States—and one of the highest in the world.

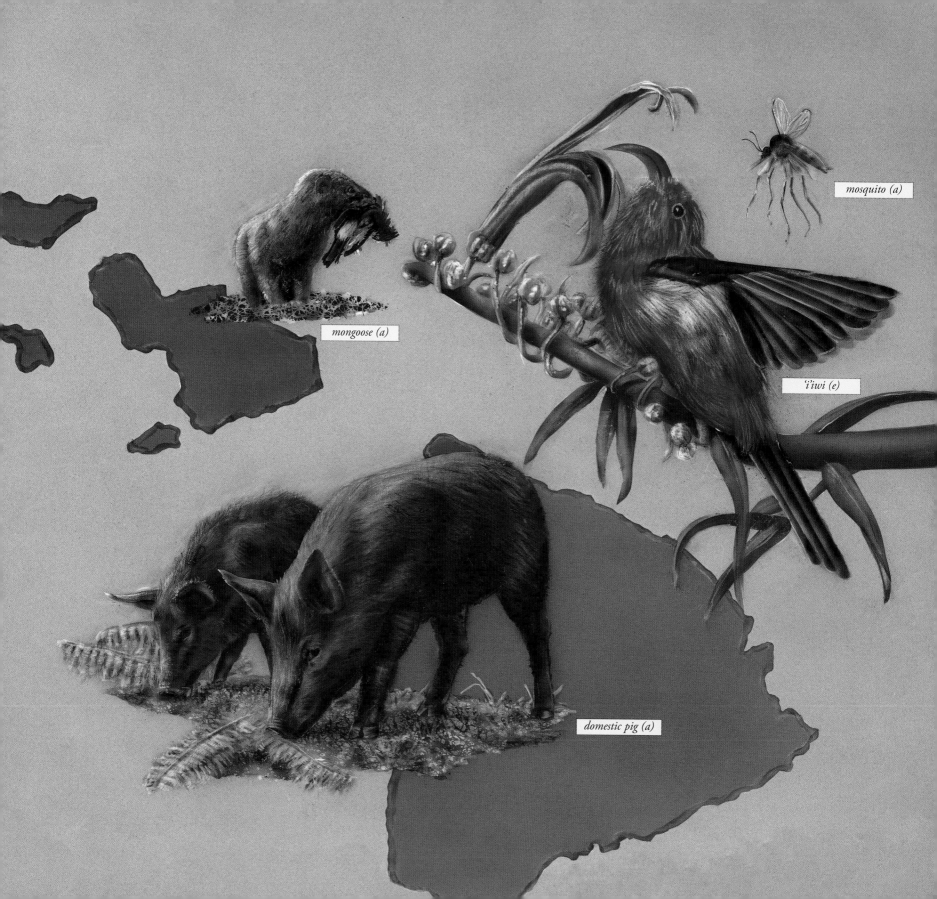

mosquito (a)

mongoose (a)

ʻiʻiwi (e)

domestic pig (a)

starling (a)

You DON'T HAVE TO live on an island to see an alien. You may find one in your own backyard.

Although they have made themselves at home, starlings were once aliens in North America. In the 1890s, a group of people in New York decided to import all the birds mentioned in Shakespeare's plays. They brought in a few pairs of starlings along with the other birds and released them in New York's Central Park. The people did not realize the problems the starlings would cause. These aggressive birds compete with native birds for food and take over the nests of some species. There are now about 200 million starlings throughout the United States.

Starlings also transmit a number of diseases that can affect humans, poultry, and livestock. Researchers have discovered that these birds sometimes carry a form of *E. coli* bacteria that can cause sickness in humans and other animals. The droppings of an infected bird can contaminate cattle feed and city environments.

gypsy moth larvae suspended on silk threads (a)

gypsy moth caterpillar (a)

SOMETIMES PEOPLE IMPORT an alien species for research, and then, despite precautions, an accident occurs and the aliens enter the native population.

Étienne Trouvelot, a French scientist who lived in Massachusetts, brought the first gypsy moths from Europe into the United States in 1869. He hoped to use them to breed a new kind of silkworm. Some of the gypsy moths escaped. Without many predators, the gypsy moth population exploded.

In its caterpillar stage, the moth can eat the leaves from more than 300 different kinds of trees. Since 1980, gypsy moths have destroyed over a million acres of forest each year. The moth has spread beyond New England to southern Canada, west to Wisconsin, and south as far as North Carolina.

It is easy for the gypsy moth to travel. Its eggs can be transported on cars, lawn furniture, tents, backpacks, firewood, or anything that is used outdoors—even the soles of people's boots.

SOME ALIEN SPECIES were introduced entirely by accident.

Exotic fire ants came from South America, arriving by cargo ship at the port of Mobile, Alabama, in the late 1930s. Without any predators, their population grew quickly. These destructive aliens cause billions of dollars in damage each year. They can ruin air conditioners and electrical equipment, and they can damage many kinds of crops, including corn and soybeans. The burning sting of the fire ant can blind and even kill young livestock and wildlife.

Fire ants have replaced two native ant species. They have now invaded more than a dozen southern and western states and spread as far west as California.

swallow (n)

fire ants (a)

leopard frog (n)

freshwater minnow (n)

zebra mussel (a)

zebra mussels attached to freshwater mussels (a)

crayfish (n)

MANY ALIENS ARRIVE in the ballast tanks on cargo ships. These large tanks of seawater, which help ships stay afloat, are like aquariums in the middle of the ship. When a ship arrives in port, it dumps its ballast tank, emptying thousands of sea urchins, worms, clams, snails, and other creatures into an ecosystem where they do not belong.

This is how zebra mussels traveled from Europe to the United States. Since arriving on cargo ships in the late 1980s, the zebra mussel has spread throughout the Great Lakes and to lakes and rivers beyond in twenty-nine states. Considered one of the most destructive invasive species in North America, huge populations of these fingernail-sized mussels live on rocks, concrete, wood, and metal. They sink buoys, clog water-intake pipes, and eat the plankton on which local fish depend.

With no predators, zebra mussels spread rapidly. A female can lay up to 500,000 eggs each year. There are now so many zebra mussels that it is impossible to get rid of them without harming other wildlife. The United States has enacted regulations to control the dumping of ballast water.

brown tree snake (a)

NATIVE TO THE SOUTH PACIFIC, the brown tree snake was accidentally introduced to the island of Guam in the 1940s in a U.S. military cargo ship. With no predators on the island, the snake spread rapidly. There are now an estimated two million of these snakes on the island. They feed on bird and reptile eggs, birds, lizards, and small mammals such as rats, mice, and small house pets. Over the years, the brown tree snake has eaten most of Guam's native birds into extinction and reduced the numbers of seabirds.

In addition to harming Guam's wildlife, brown tree snakes climb power lines and get into transformers and electrical boxes, causing hundreds of power outages and costing the island millions of dollars each year.

In an attempt to reduce the snake population, the U.S. has dropped dead mice laced with the common painkiller, acetaminophen, into Guam's rainforest canopy. When the snakes eat the mice, the medicine blocks the ability of the snake's blood to carry oxygen throughout its body, causing them to die. This method won't get rid of all the alien brown tree snakes, but it will help control the numbers in the rainforest.

Mariana fruit dove (n)

green anole (n)

domestic cattle (n)

kudzu (a)

ALIEN PLANTS CAN also become invasive and destructive to native habitats.

When people introduced kudzu to the United States, they had good intentions. The Japanese brought the fast-growing vine to decorate their exhibit at the 1876 Centennial Exposition in Philadelphia, Pennsylvania. Americans liked the beautiful green vine with its sweet-smelling blossoms and began planting it in their gardens.

In the 1930s, the U.S. government, hoping to save some of the farmland that was being lost to erosion in the southeastern states, hired hundreds of workers to plant kudzu. People believed that the vine would help to prevent soil from being washed away during rains.

No one realized that the warm, humid climate was even more suitable for kudzu than that of its native Japan. Today, this vine, which can grow up to a foot a day, covers more than seven million acres in the southeastern U. S. It destroys forests by covering trees and preventing them from getting sunlight.

Despite efforts to control the vine by mowing, applying herbicides, or using various biological agents, kudzu continues to spread.

dingo (a)

cane toad (a)

SOMETIMES WELL-MEANING people import an alien species to get rid of a local pest.

In the 1930s, beetles were damaging sugarcane fields in Australia, the United States, and other countries. People imported cane toads—large, insect-eating amphibians—from South America to eat the beetles. But the toads ignored the beetles and ate human garbage and pet food instead. The poison secreted from special glands on the toads' shoulders killed dogs, cats, snakes, and other animals that preyed on the toads. The people who had imported the toads realized that now they had an even bigger problem.

Another similar experiment of the 1930s ended in failure. To bring a growing population of rats under control, Micronesian farmers brought in giant monitor lizards. Because the rats are nighttime animals and monitor lizards are daytime creatures, they didn't encounter one another. Rather than eating the rats, the lizards ate the islanders' chickens. In an effort to control the lizards, the Micronesians imported the cane toad. The toad population increased, leading to the poisoning of cats and dogs, animals that had once been fairly effective in keeping the rats in check. In the end, the farmers were worse off than they had been before the start of the experiment.

young giant monitor lizard (a)

giant monitor lizard (a)

cane toad (a)

IN THE 1970S, U.S. government agencies introduced several species of Asian carp—including black, silver, grass, and bighead—to control weeds and parasites in fish farm ponds.

These types of carp eat up to a fifth of their body weight in plants every day and can reach a size of 100 pounds. Without predators, Asian carp spread into waterways along the Mississippi River basin and reproduced rapidly, damaging the habitat of native fish and shellfish and consuming the plankton and vegetation those species depend on for survival. The carp sometimes prey on native species of mussels, snails, larval fish, and some adult fish. Silver carp can also be a hazard to humans. These powerful fish often jump out of the water and into boats, causing accidents.

In an effort to keep the carp out of the Great Lakes, officials have created an underwater electrical field between the Mississippi River and Lake Michigan. It is now illegal to import Asian carp or transport these fish between states without a permit.

Asian carp (a)

iguana (a)

painted turtle (a)

SOME PEOPLE ILLEGALLY CARRY exotic animals across borders to sell or to keep as pets. Customs officials have found iguanas, electric eels, snapping turtles, hamsters, parrots, and other animals in luggage, shoe boxes, and plastic bowls. Smuggling exotic animals not only introduces aliens into a new habitat, but also may deplete the native populations of certain species.

Whenever you enter the United States after a trip, customs officials ask if you are carrying any animal, plant, or food from the country you have been visiting. Even the tiniest piece of fruit can carry an alien insect that could cause huge damage in a new habitat.

Alien species can now hitch a fast, free ride with humans. Whenever we travel anywhere, we need to take care that we do not carry alien invaders with us.

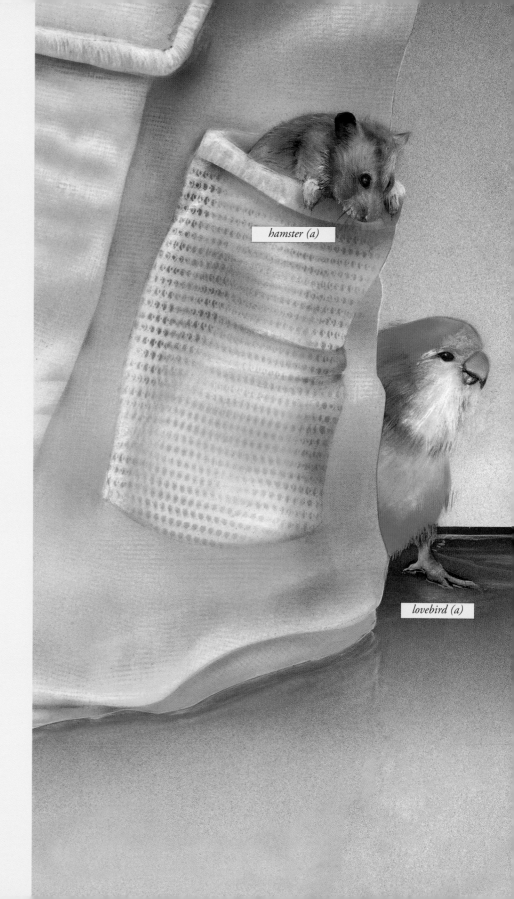

hamster (a)

lovebird (a)

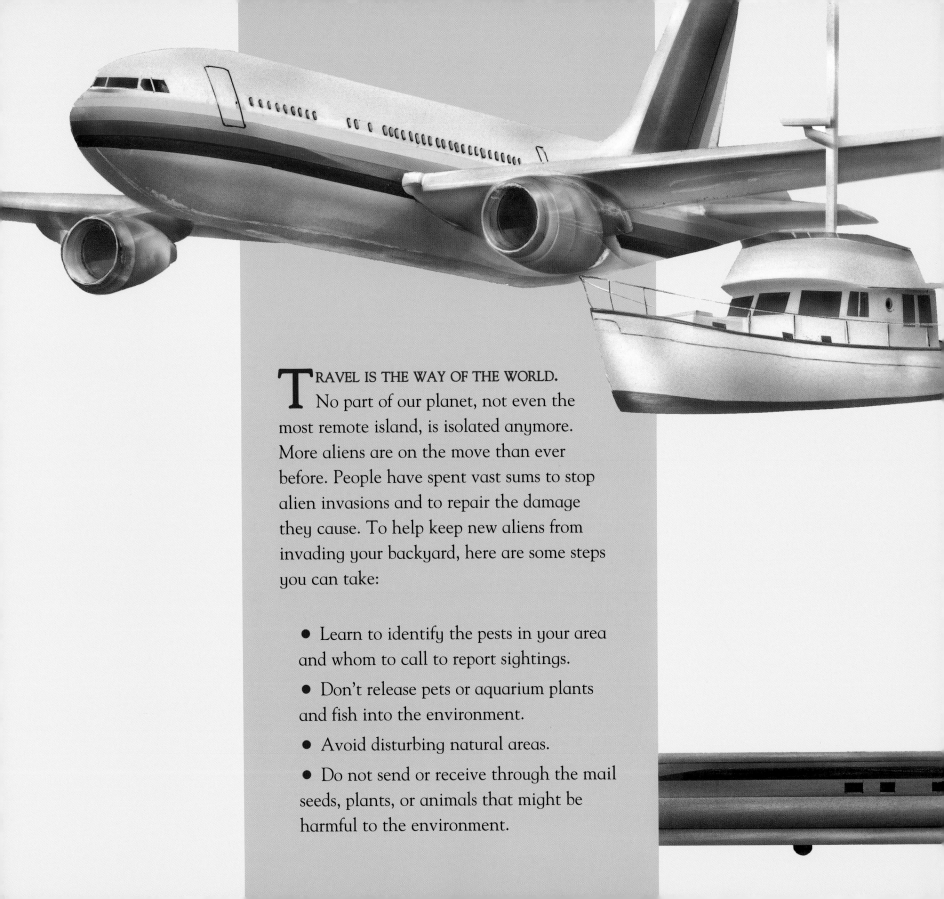

TRAVEL IS THE WAY OF THE WORLD. No part of our planet, not even the most remote island, is isolated anymore. More aliens are on the move than ever before. People have spent vast sums to stop alien invasions and to repair the damage they cause. To help keep new aliens from invading your backyard, here are some steps you can take:

- Learn to identify the pests in your area and whom to call to report sightings.

- Don't release pets or aquarium plants and fish into the environment.

- Avoid disturbing natural areas.

- Do not send or receive through the mail seeds, plants, or animals that might be harmful to the environment.

- When you and your family travel, do not bring plants, fruits, soil, seeds, or animals into your country from abroad.

- Clean your boats and boating equipment before taking them from one body of water to another. Leave behind any unused bait and bucket water.

- Clean your boots and camping gear before going to another area or country, and again before returning home.

- Learn more about invasive species by reading books and articles and by checking websites like *www.invasivespecies.gov.*

The place where you live is your habitat. You share it with many different kinds of animals and plants. Help protect them, yourself, and Earth's biodiversity from alien invaders.

GLOSSARY

biodiversity: The variety of different plants and animals and ecosystems that make up life on Earth.

community: All the organisms—plants, animals, and microorganisms—that live together in a particular place, such as a forest or a seashore.

ecosystem: A community of plants and animals living in balance with each other and with their environment. An ecosystem can be a small like a pond or large like the ocean or the entire planet.

endangered species: A group of animals or plants that are at risk of extinction (according to the Endangered Species Act of 1973).

environment: The surroundings and conditions—including water, light, soil, food sources, and other organisms—that affect the growth and development of living things.

extinct: No longer existing in living form.

habitat: The particular environment where a plant or animal normally lives and grows.

migration: The long-distance movement of living things from one region to another.

organism: Any living thing.

parasite: An organism that lives in or on a different organism, called a host, from which it gets food. Parasites are often harmful to the host.

population: All the organisms of a species living in a certain area.

predator: An animal that lives by hunting and feeding upon other animals.

prey: Animals that are hunted and eaten by other animals.

species: A group of closely related animals or plants that can breed with one another in nature.

threatened species: A group of animals or plants that are at risk of becoming endangered (according to the Endangered Species Act of 1973).

FOR FURTHER READING

Burdick, Alan. *Out of Eden: An Odyssey of Ecological Invasion.* Farrar, Straus, and Giroux, 2006.

*Collard, Sneed B. *Science Warriors: The Battle Against Invasive Species* (Scientists in the Field Series). HMH Books for Young Readers, 2008.

Davis, Mark A. *Invasion Biology.* Oxford University Press, USA, 2009.

Hamilton, Garry. *Super Species: The Creatures That Will Dominate the Planet.* Firefly Books, Ltd., 2010.

Hardy, Sarah Blaffer. *Mothers and Others: The Evolutionary Origins of Mutual Understanding.* The Belknap Press of Harvard University Press, 2009.

"Invasive Species." *Time Magazine.* July 28, 2014.

Kolbert, Elizabeth. *The Sixth Extinction: An Unnatural History.* Henry Holt & Co., 2014.

*Latta, Sara L. *Keep Out: Invasive Species.* Capstone Press, 2013.

Marris, Emma. *Rambunctious Garden: Saving Nature in a Post-Wild World.* Bloomsbury USA, 2013.

*O'Connor, Karen. *The Threat of Invasive Species.* Gareth Stevens Publishing, 2013.

Of interest for younger readers

WEBSITES

www.doi.gov//invasivespecies/index.cfm

www.fws.gov/invasives/

www.invasivespeciesinfo.gov

water.epa.gov/type/oceb/habitat/invasive_species_index.cfm

AUTHOR'S NOTE

INVASIVE SPECIES are not going away. It's a global problem and it's serious, impacting the environment, agriculture, and human health. Each year more alien plants, animals, and microbes invade ecosystems around the world. At the same time, climate change, with warming land and ocean temperatures, is expanding the ranges of species. Since the first edition of this book was published in 2003, the noxious weed kudzu, which was once confined to the southeastern states in the U.S., has now moved northward to Ohio and Ontario, Canada. Without severe winters, which kill their larvae, pine bark beetle populations have exploded across the western U.S., killing billions of trees.

By 2050, warmer winters are predicted to expand the range of the deer tick that carries Lyme disease into several central states and parts of southern Canada. Tropical diseases like malaria and dengue fever may become more prevalent as the mosquitoes carrying these ailments expand their ranges farther north. According to the Smithsonian Environmental Research Center, the melting of Arctic sea ice is connecting two oceans—the north Pacific and north Atlantic—that had been separated for some two million years, creating a passage for a massive wave of invasive species.

You never hear of many invasive species because they fit into ecosystems without causing damage. But the invasive species that

become troublesome pests can not only carry diseases, they can also wreak havoc by out-competing or preying on native species, often driving them into extinction. Globally, they are the second leading cause of species endangerment, and efforts to control them are costly. According to the U.S. Department of Agriculture, as of 2015, invasive pests cost the U.S. $120 billion each year. Most states and countries have invasive species management programs to eradicate the pests if possible, and to control those—like zebra and quagga mussels—whose populations have exploded beyond any possibility of eradicating them.

In some cases, such as the infestation of the fast-growing invasive seaweed *Caulerpa taxifolia* in southern California, eradication has been successful. In the case of Africanized bees, beekeepers learned to manage them safely, so they haven't become the frightening "killer bee" menace initially predicted and hyped by Hollywood.

The best protection against invasive species is knowledge. Learn to tell the difference between real science and media hype. Educate yourself about the invasive species in your county or state. Invasive species are now everybody's problem; we all share the same planetary backyard.

—*Mary Batten*